Hillsboro Public Library
Hillsboro, OR
A member of Washington County
COOPERATIVE LIBRARY SERVICES

Mindfulness

— in —

Nature

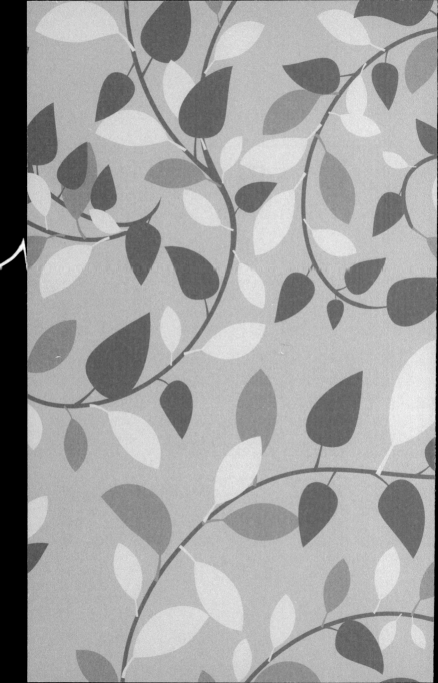

Mindfulness
—in—
Nature

Nina Smiley and David Harp

hatherleigh
Improve your life. Change your world.

Hatherleigh Press is committed to preserving and protecting the natural resources of the earth. Environmentally responsible and sustainable practices are embraced within the company's mission statement.

Visit us at www.hatherleighpress.com and register online for free offers, discounts, special events, and more.

Mindfulness in Nature
Text copyright © 2017 Nina Smiley and David Harp

Quotes on pages 31 and 33 from *The Sense of Wonder* by Rachel Carson
Copyright © 1956 by Rachel L. Carson
Reprinted by permission of Frances Collin, Trustee

33614080202723

Library of Congress Cataloging-in-Publication Data
is available upon request.
ISBN: 978-1-57826-676-0

All rights reserved. No part of this book may be reproduced, stored in a retrieval system, or transmitted, in any form or by any means, electronic or otherwise, without written permission from the publisher.

Interior Design by Cynthia Dunne

Printed in the United States
10 9 8 7 6 5 4 3 2 1

Contents

❦

Publisher's Note:
The Gift of Mindfulness

❧

"Lose yourself in nature and find peace."

RALPH WALDO EMERSON

I have been fortunate to hike the trails of Mohonk, climb its cliffs, and swim its icy streams for most of my adult life.

Living in New York City, Mohonk presented me with the ideal opportunity to escape to nature, less than two hours from my urban home. The breath of life gained by experiencing these woods and wilds and the impressive geologic upheaval of the escarpment opened my visual senses, and was essential for surviving the city and its manmade vistas.

Now more than ever, with the constant distractions that abound in modern life—from smart phones to social media—it is absolutely imperative that we be able to seek the solace and comfort of nature. And not only for our own health and well-being—even more so for the betterment of us all. For it is by partaking in nature that we come to understand our imperative: to preserve our environs for the generations that follow.

In these pages, you will find the wisdom and inspiration to step out of our artificial spaces and bathe in the canopy of nature that stretches from forest to sea, from earth to sky and through to the stars. Welcome this opportunity, and rediscover and restore your connection with the Eternal.

—Andrew Flach, Publisher

Introduction

To seek mindfulness in nature is a meaningful part of the human experience. Delighting in the natural world, being struck by a sense of awe at the transcendent power of nature, and feeling nurtured by its depth of healing are timeless sentiments.

Mindfulness is simply a state that involves being aware of our thoughts, feelings, and surroundings in any given moment, in a gentle, non-judgmental way. In recent years, huge numbers of scientific studies have shown how a "mindfulness meditation practice" can reduce stress and enhance daily life in a myriad of ways.

Meditation is the tool or exercise that produces the state of mindfulness. Meditating just means that we practice keeping our mental attention tightly focused on *any* object of our choice. The best known objects for meditation are one's own breath, or a "mantra" (a specific repeated sound or phrase).

However, for thousands of years, poets, scientists, and philosophers have been using nature (including the remarkable universe of flora, fauna, mountains, oceans, and cosmos that surround us) as a meditation object with which to build mindfulness, and obtain its benefits. Hence this book.

We can feel the healing power of nature every time we step outdoors, if we can be mindfully open to the moment and are willing to be truly present in the experience with body, mind, and spirit. The combination of mindfulness with nature offers a wonderful opportunity to explore a centered, calm, and joyful state of being.

Close your eyes for a moment and bring to mind how you felt the last time you recall being *truly present* in nature. Perhaps it was on vacation at a spectacular natural setting, viewing a canyon carved into a wall of rock, or walking through a forest that shaded and surrounded you. Or perhaps it was simply stepping outdoors on a day when the air first felt like spring. Pausing to center within and enjoy this recollection may bring up a sense of spaciousness, stillness, connectedness, and well-being that goes beyond words.

Using nature as a metaphor to deepen our understanding of how we relate to ourselves, each other, and the world, this book seeks to provide inspiration and to suggest simple actions that will help weave the power of mindfulness and of nature into daily life.

Each one of us has the opportunity to choose in each moment to be mindful and to use nature as a touchstone that will center and support us, uplifting body, mind, and spirit.

How to Use This Book

I n this small book, we explain how to use nature as a meditation practice to renew and refresh yourself, anywhere and anytime.

The quotes in Part I offer a collection of mindful moments inspired by nature, as seen through the eyes of poets, writers, naturalists, philosophers, and scientists across the ages. We invite you to ponder them, whether outdoors in a natural setting, upon waking in the morning, or inside before bedtime. Reflecting on these words brings the spacious and nurturing presence of nature into the moment, no matter where you are with this book as a companion. Or, you can bring your favorite lines with you.

In Part II, some of our favorite quotes have inspired simple exercises that we hope you will bring into your life. Chosen to nurture an understanding of applying mindfulness to nature, as well as to deepen a sense of awe, each quotation invites you to take a few minutes to reflect and renew. We hope you will explore these with a sense of adventure and delight.

May this book help you welcome mindfulness, nature, and enhanced well-being into your life, one moment at a time.

"Mindfulness"
in Languages around
the World

❦

Phrases for "mindfulness" and for "love of nature" exist in many languages!

aldhdhahan	Arabic
vnimatelnost	Bulgarian
zhèngniàn	Chinese
pleine conscience	French
achtsamkeit	German
chuibuka-sa	Japanese
tankefullhet	Norwegian
uwaznosc	Polish
osoznannost'	Russian
atención plena	Spanish
farkındalık	Turkish

"Love of Nature" in Languages around the World

Hubb alttabiea	Arabic
Lyubovta na Prirodata	Bulgarian
Rè'ài dà zìrán	Chinese
L'amour de la nature	French
Liebe der Natur	German
Shizen no ai	Japanese
Kjærlighet til naturena	Norwegian
Miłosc do natury	Polish
Lyubov' k prirode	Russian
Amor de la naturaleza	Spanish
Doğa sevgisi	Turkish

PART I

Through the Ages:

Mindful Moments

and Nature

On the pages that follow, you will find quotes inspired by the beauty, grandeur, mystery, and simplicity of nature.

These thoughts from writers, naturalists, poets, artists, and philosophers across the centuries—and even millennia—are a tribute to the power of nature to expand our hearts and minds.

Nature calls forth in us a joy that elevates ordinary moments, and a humility that offers a touchstone for understanding the Universe, as it simultaneously centers us deeply in the moment.

As you read these pages, take time to pause and reflect on the role that mindfulness in nature has, or might have, in the context of your life.

The clearest way into the Universe is through a forest wilderness.

JOHN MUIR

There is pleasure in the pathless woods, there is rapture in the lonely shore, there is society where none intrudes, by the deep sea, and music in its roar; I love not Man the less, but Nature more.

LORD BYRON

Nature offers unceasingly the most novel and fascinating objects for learning.

ALEXANDER VON HUMBOLDT

To sit in the shade on a fine day, and look upon verdure, is the most perfect refreshment.

JANE AUSTEN

If I spent enough time with the tiniest creature—even a caterpillar—I would never have to prepare a sermon. So full of God is every creature.

MEISTER ECKHART

The subtlety of nature is greater many times over than the subtlety of the senses and understanding.

FRANCIS BACON

I can enjoy society in a room; but out of doors, nature is company enough for me.

WILLIAM HAZLITT

Heaven is under our feet as well as over our heads.

HENRY DAVID THOREAU

My miserable hearing does not trouble me here. In the country it seems as if every tree said to me: 'Holy! Holy!' Who can give complete expression to the ecstasy of the woods! O, the sweet stillness of the woods!

LUDWIG VAN BEETHOVEN

To the mind that is still, the whole universe surrenders.

LAO TZU

I loafe and invite my soul,
I lean and loafe at my ease observing a spear of
summer grass.

WALT WHITMAN

Nature is what we know—yet have not art to say—
So impotent our wisdom is to her simplicity.

EMILY DICKINSON

Nature understands no jesting; she is always true, always serious, always severe; she is always right, and the errors and faults are always those of man.

JOHANN WOLFGANG VON GOETHE

I wonder if the snow loves the trees and fields, that it kisses them so gently? And then it covers them up snug, you know, with a white quilt; and perhaps it says 'Go to sleep, darlings, till the summer comes again.'

LEWIS CARROLL

Among the scenes which are deeply impressed on my mind, none exceeded in sublimity the primeval forests undefaced by the hand of man.

CHARLES DARWIN

If you live according to nature, you never will be poor;
if according to the world's caprice, you will never
be rich.

PUBLILIUS SYRUS

The lack of power to take joy in outdoor nature is
as real a misfortune as the lack of power to take joy
in books.

THEODORE ROOSEVELT

What is a weed?
A plant whose virtues have yet to be discovered.

RALPH WALDO EMERSON

I go to nature to be soothed and healed, and to have my senses put in order.

JOHN BURROUGHS

A thing of beauty is a joy forever.

JOHN KEATS

And this, our life, exempt from public haunt, finds tongues in trees, books in the running brooks, sermons in stones, and good in everything.

WILLIAM SHAKESPEARE

It is not so much for its beauty that the forest makes a claim upon men's hearts, as for that subtle something, that quality of air that emanation from old trees, that so wonderfully changes and renews a weary spirit.

ROBERT LOUIS STEVENSON

Nature can do more than physicians.

OLIVER CROMWELL

When one tugs at a single thing in nature, he finds it attached to the rest of the world.

JOHN MUIR

Summer afternoon; to me those have always been the two most beautiful words in the English language.

HENRY JAMES

The tree which moves some to tears of joy is in the eyes of others only a green thing that stands in the way. Some see nature all ridicule and deformity... and some scarce see nature at all. But to the eyes of the man of imagination, nature is imagination itself.

WILLIAM BLAKE

Nature has spread for us a rich and delightful banquet. Shall we turn from it?

THOMAS COLE

Nature gives to every time and season some beauties of its own.

CHARLES DICKENS

Every particular in nature, a leaf, a drop, a crystal, a moment of time is related to the whole, and partakes of the perfection of the whole.

RALPH WALDO EMERSON

Nature! We are surrounded and embraced by her: powerless to separate ourselves from her...

T.H. HUXLEY

Here and elsewhere we shall not obtain the best insight into things until we actually see them growing from the beginning.

ARISTOTLE

Long before I learned to do a sum in arithmetic or describe the shape of the earth, Miss Sullivan had taught me to find beauty in the fragrant woods, in every blade of grass...

HELEN KELLER

All art is but imitation of nature.

SENECA

Nature is an infinite sphere of which the center is everywhere and the circumference nowhere.

BLAISE PASCAL

There are no words that can tell the hidden spirit of the wilderness, that can reveal its mystery, its melancholy, and its charm.

THEODORE ROOSEVELT

Nature is painting for us, day after day, pictures of infinite beauty, if only we have the eyes to see them.

JOHN RUSKIN

The earth has received the embrace of the sun and we shall see the results of that love.

SITTING BULL

Words, like nature, half reveal and half conceal the soul within.

ALFRED LORD TENNYSON

Live in each season as it passes; breathe the air, drink the drink, taste the fruit, and resign yourself to the influence of the earth.

HENRY DAVID THOREAU

If I were to name the three most precious resources of life, I should say books, friends, and nature; and the greatest of these, at least the most constant and always at hand, is nature.

JOHN BURROUGHS

Nature, whose sweet rains fall on unjust and just alike, will have clefts in the rocks where I may hide, and secret valleys in whose silence I may weep undisturbed.

OSCAR WILDE

To me a lush carpet of pine needles or spongy grass is more welcome than the most luxurious Persian rug.

HELEN KELLER

Let Nature be your teacher.

WILLIAM WORDSWORTH

Keep a green bough in your heart and a singing bird will come.

LAO TZU

Let the clean air blow the cobwebs from your body. Air is medicine.

LILLIAN RUSSELL

Those who contemplate the beauty of the earth find reserves of strength that will endure as long as life lasts. There is something infinitely healing in the repeated refrains of nature—the assurance that dawn comes after night, and spring after winter.

RACHEL CARSON

All my life I have tried to pluck a thistle and plant a flower wherever the flower would grow in thought and mind.

ABRAHAM LINCOLN

To the artist there is never anything ugly in nature.

AUGUSTE RODIN

Even kings and emperors with heaps of wealth and vast dominion cannot compare with an ant filled with the love of God.

GURU NANAK

Flowers are the sweetest things that God ever made and forgot to put a soul into.

HENRY WARD BEECHER

Don't live by your own rules, but in harmony with nature.

EPICTETUS

It is not half so important to know as to feel when introducing a young child to the natural world.

RACHEL CARSON

I might mention all the divine charms of a bright spring day, but if you had never in your life utterly forgotten yourself in straining your eyes after the mounting lark, or in wandering through the still lanes when the fresh-opened blossoms fill them with a sacred silent beauty like that of fretted aisles, where would be the use of my descriptive catalogue?

GEORGE ELIOT (MARY ANNE EVANS)

Nature is always new in the spring, and lucky are we if it finds us new also.

JOHN BURROUGHS

Remind thyself that he whom thou lovest is mortal, that what thou lovest is not thine own; it is given thee for the present, not irrevocably nor forever, but even as a fig or a bunch of grapes at the appointed season of the year.

EPICTETUS

Nature's peace will flow into you as sunshine flows into trees.

JOHN MUIR

Every leaf speaks bliss to me
Fluttering from the autumn tree.

EMILY BRONTË

I'd give all the wealth that years have piled, the slow
results of life's decay,
To be once more a little child for one bright summer
day.

LEWIS CARROLL

I would wish that all young persons might be exhorted
to read the great book of nature, wherein they may see
the wisdom and power of the Creator, in the order of
the universe, and in the production of all things.

ANNE BAYNARD

To the lover of birds, insects, and plants, the smallest area around a well-chosen home will furnish sufficient material to satisfy all thirst of knowledge through the longest life.

MARY TREAT

...a traveller should be a botanist, for in all views plants form the chief embellishment.

CHARLES DARWIN

How came the bodies of animals to be contrived with so much art, and for what ends were their several parts? Was the eye contrived without skill in Opticks, and the ear without knowledge of sounds?

ISAAC NEWTON

Give me solitude—give me Nature—give me again,
O Nature, your primal sanities!]

WALT WHITMAN

Nature is a revelation of God; Art is a revelation of man.

HENRY WADSWORTH LONGFELLOW

Climb the mountains and get their good tidings.
Nature's peace will flow into you as sunshine flows into
trees. The winds will blow their own freshness into
you, and the storms their energy, while cares will drop
off like autumn leaves.

JOHN MUIR

The poetry of the earth is never dead.

JOHN KEATS

Keep your love of nature, for that is the true way to understand art more and more.

VINCENT VAN GOGH

The sun shines not on us but in us.

JOHN MUIR

A man is related to all nature.

RALPH WALDO EMERSON

One touch of nature makes the whole world kin.

WILLIAM SHAKESPEARE

In the spring, I have counted 136 different kinds of weather inside of 24 hours.

MARK TWAIN

PART II

Exploring Mindfulness

in Nature:

Seeking Simplicity,

Experiencing Awe

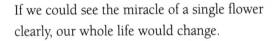

If we could see the miracle of a single flower
clearly, our whole life would change.

THE BUDDHA

2,500 YEARS AGO, SIDDHARTHA Gautama, known as the Buddha, began to develop a mental and spiritual discipline that has come to be known as mindfulness meditation. The connection between mindfulness and nature was beautifully stated when he noted how being fully present with the "miracle" of a single flower could change our understanding of the world.

Although seeing just one flower clearly is harder than it might seem, there's a simplicity at the heart of the Buddha's suggestion that makes this approachable. We don't need to take a month off to trek in the Himalayas, or hike the Appalachian Trail. We simply need to be willing to learn how to focus our attention and be fully present in any given moment, mindfully aware of our thoughts, feelings, and surroundings.

Opportunities to be mindful in nature

abound, yet sometimes we are distracted and unable to notice or recognize such moments as they occur. As with anything we seek to learn, we need to practice this new behavior of being mindful, and we need to make time for the small efforts that, cumulatively, have the power to change our whole life.

In this section, you'll find suggestions that invite mindfulness—and mindfulness in nature—into your life on a daily basis. They will take only a few minutes and you will find that this practice can fit seamlessly into your life. As you practice, let yourself experience the sense of spaciousness, well-being, and connection that comes when you deepen your understanding of the natural world, and enhance your connection to those who inhabit it. As you embrace this new awareness, you'll find that this shift can bring joy to your life, day by day and moment to moment.

As a single footstep will not make a path on the earth, so a single thought will not make a pathway in the mind. To make a deep physical path, we walk again and again. To make a deep mental path, we must think over and over the kind of thoughts we wish to dominate our lives.

HENRY DAVID THOREAU

THIS IMAGE OF WALKING in nature beautifully captures what science has come to understand about how the mind works. Our brains are composed of cells called *neurons* that link together to form *neural paths* that underlie all of our actions, thoughts, and emotions.

Every time we do, think, or feel something new, a neural path is formed. Every time that path is used or even remembered, more neurons join to make the neural path thicker and more easily "travelled." Much of a mindfulness practice involves noticing and identifying our most common neural paths so that we can begin to *choose* where to place our attention.

Pay attention to thoughts that arise. As with favorite paths which we choose to walk repeatedly in nature, we can choose the neural paths that we deepen by repetition in our brains. Resolve to strengthen neural paths for actions, thoughts, and feelings that enhance your well-being and let go of those that create unhappiness or stress.

Everything has beauty, but not everyone sees it.

CONFUCIUS

E VEN OUTDOORS IN THE grandeur of nature, there may be times when we're so preoccupied with our thoughts that we're barely aware of the world around us.

Becoming aware that our attention has been hijacked—often to fears, desires, or other emotions—can become the base for a practice of mindfulness that will help us learn to control our attention and avoid getting stuck in a mental fog.

Being able to notice the flowers means being able to focus on good and beautiful things in life, even when things are not going well and we are likely to be focused on negative thoughts. Being able to momentarily pay attention to, and appreciate, the beautiful and the good applies to all aspects of life.

Today be aware of the "flowers in your life" and take a moment to savor and enjoy them.

In all things of nature, there is something marvelous.

ARISTOTLE

N ATURE IS ALL AROUND us, if we're willing to perceive it. From the sunlight we feel on our skin as we
walk down a canyon path or a busy urban street, to the
raindrops that catch us unaware, to the grass growing
through the cracks in a concrete sidewalk, nature offers
opportunities to marvel at *each moment*, when we are
mindfully present in the experience.

Outdoors or indoors, whether on a bustling city street
or in the country, practice noticing the natural world.
Pay close attention to what you perceive. Do so without judgment, without telling yourself a story about it in
words. Do you see it? Hear it? Smell it? Feel it on your
skin?

Whether you call this immersion "forest bathing" or
"mindfulness in nature"—simply observe, carefully, with
all your senses. As you do so, be in touch with the wonder of the moment. Feel your sense of connection with
the natural world expand. Feel the joy that comes with
this connection, no matter where you are.

The best thing one can do when it's raining is to let it rain.

HENRY WADSWORTH LONGFELLOW

I N ADDITION TO RAIN, there are many things in life we cannot change. Nature offers us opportunities on a daily basis to explore and deepen our understanding of how a mindful approach to life can make a difference. When it rains, even if we had wanted to go out and work in the garden, we can still notice the power and beauty of the storm and appreciate the water nurturing the thirsty earth.

Mindfulness invites us to simply be present in the moment with *what is*, accept it for *what it is*, and feel compassion for our impatience, annoyance, and desire to see it be different.

When nature or life provides opportunities in which your preferences are not being met, take several slow, full breaths. Gently notice and feel each inhale and each exhale. Let go of judgmental thoughts (such as "It shouldn't be this way!" or "I hate when that happens!") and be present in the moment, appreciating the opportunity to work with mindfulness in real time.

Should you shield the canyons from the windstorms
you would never see the true beauty of their carvings.

ELISABETH KÜBLER-ROSS

I N NATURE, STORMS SHAPE the canyons to create remarkable carvings. Similarly, in daily life, we have experiences that are stressful, unanticipated, painful, and out of our control. As we appreciate the beauty that comes from upheaval or disturbance in the natural world, we can recognize that it takes the rough-and-tumble of real and even painful experiences to shape *us*, and that these events are opportunities for growth.

Each time we practice being mindfully present in the moment and address a bad mood, a stubbed toe, or a blow to our self-esteem with equanimity, we strengthen our practice, and thus make ourselves—*carve* ourselves—into a slightly more skillful person.

When something unpleasant happens, notice what's going on in your body. As the annoyance occurs, your body will probably tense up. Your jaw may clench; your breathing may get shallow. As you experience this, consciously relax your muscles and turn your attention to your breath. Soften around the stress and let it go. The more often you do this, the easier it becomes.

If you look deep enough you will see music; the heart
of nature being everywhere music.

THOMAS CARLYLE

BEING OUTDOORS IN A natural setting and being mindfully aware of your senses creates an opportunity to experience the magic of all that is.

Choose a quiet place where you can go to explore "deep listening" in nature. Whether in a garden, a park, the beach, or a neighborhood street lined with trees, spend at least ten minutes simply being present in the moment.

As you breathe gently and fully, release your thoughts and focus exclusively on the sounds around you. As you listen without mental distraction, you will likely begin to hear a tapestry of sound that was previously outside your awareness. What do you hear close by? What can you hear in the distance?

Delight in the music of the Earth as it washes over you.

To see a world in a grain of sand and heaven in a wild flower, hold infinity in the palm of your hand and eternity in an hour.

WILLIAM BLAKE

As we continue to be mindful in nature—present in the moment, in touch with our senses, and simply aware of what is—we may begin to feel a sense of spaciousness as the mind becomes clear of thoughts.

Practice being present in the moment in a natural setting that nurtures an expansiveness within you. It may be a setting with a view. It may be the tiniest part of the natural world, a single flower. Breathe gently and fully as you focus attention on it, and invite a sense of spaciousness to inform your awareness.

How might infinity feel in your mind and heart? What might eternity feel like as it embraced you?

❦ ❦ ❦

Nature does not hurry. Yet everything is accomplished.

LAO TZU

Aₛ ᴡᴇ ʟᴏᴏᴋ ᴛᴏ nature for guidance on how to live, we can see that there are insights to be drawn from the world around us. Nature has a pace all her own. From the movement of glaciers that shaped the earliest years of our planet to the planting of trees in the spring, nature has a time-frame that encompasses all.

If you feel rushed and stressed, take a slow, full, mindful breath and remind yourself that there is a flow to getting things done. Become aware that rushing and multi-tasking are more often detriments to life than enhancements to it.

As you continue to breathe slowly, deeply, fully, you can align yourself with the energy of the process you've begun. As we recognize nature as our model, we understand that mindful, focused energy will help us to complete our tasks more easily than frenetic haste.

🍃 🍃 🍃

Nature never deceives us.
It is we who deceive ourselves.

JEAN-JACQUES ROUSSEAU

If we see nature clearly—with eyes that perceive the reality of each moment, a mind that is free from preconceptions and incessant self-talk, and a heart that is open to all that is—nature will never deceive us.

Acknowledging that we deceive ourselves is a profound opportunity for insight. It means acknowledging our human frailties and recognizing that we may misperceive incoming information or filter it through a protective lens, or even a negative one.

Become aware if there are times when you may be deceiving yourself. As you interact with others or spend time alone, watch the mind to see if it is creating "stories" that move beyond fact. If you become aware of such stories, you can begin to ask yourself, "is this true?" and to hold the answers gently, while allowing them to inform your subsequent thoughts and actions.

❦ ❦ ❦

Earth laughs in flowers.

RALPH WALDO EMERSON

As we spend time in nature, we find we become more attuned to the intent of the natural world. We begin to understand the ebb and flow of sunlight, the rise and fall of the moon.

From the sparseness of winter, to the renewal of spring, to the abundance of summer flowers, to the changing colors of fall, we delight in the seasons.

As you see flowers in real life or in images, feel the joy of the Earth. Feel the lightness and laughter in each flower's natural beauty and spend a moment appreciating the wonder of the natural world.

🌿 🌿 🌿

We do not see nature with our eyes, but with our understandings and our hearts.

WILLIAM HAZLITT

BEING MINDFUL IN NATURE calls upon all of our senses and then moves beyond. Through seeing and hearing, using senses of touch, smell, and taste, we find ourselves opening to the moment as we explore the physical dimensions of nature's grandeur and beauty, and then move beyond words.

Simply be present and experience how it feels to be in a natural setting without using words. Take the miracle of nature into your heart and your deepest understanding. As you quiet your mind and let nature speak directly to your soul, you nurture your deepest well-being.

❦ ❦ ❦

Nature will bear the closest inspection. She invites us to lay our eye level with her smallest leaf, and take an insect view of its plain.

HENRY DAVID THOREAU

I⊤'s EASY TO KEEP our attention focused on the newest TV series, or a fast-breaking story on the Internet. But we don't build "mental muscle" by looking at things that we're used to. Instead, if we spend some time practicing Thoreau's "close attention," we can increase our power to focus our mental attention exactly where we want it, and when we want it.

We do so by honing our attentional skills on less than intrinsically attractive things, like the insect-eye view of a single leaf. Or the carefully observed and detailed process of a single breath as it enters, fills the body, and then leaves, with subtle sensations throughout.

This kind of practice helps us to avoid un-useful thoughts, whether they are judgments, desires, fears, angers, or any other unskillful mental objects that will fill our minds, if we allow them to.

Sunshine is delicious, rain is refreshing, wind braces us up, snow is exhilarating; there is really no such thing as bad weather, only different kinds of good weather.

JOHN RUSKIN

OFTEN WITHOUT REALIZING IT, we find ourselves running a mental commentary on people, events, and things around us. When we do become aware of this internal monologue, we may be surprised at how often it is negative. Minds are used to judging: good, bad, right, wrong. Yet, when we're being mindful, there's also the possibility of *simply observing*.

Watch the thoughts that run through your mind and become aware of the stream of commentary. Notice if it's negative, neutral, or positive. Starting as simply as observing your reactions to the weather, become aware that your thoughts shape your feelings. Choose to let go of "judging thoughts" and feel your emotions lighten with this mental shift.

If you truly love nature, you'll find beauty everywhere.

Vincent van Gogh

Understanding that "beauty lies in the eyes of the beholder," as Plato noted long ago, offers an opportunity for us to take responsibility for becoming mindful beholders. In order to delight in the beauty and joy of nature, and in the freshness of each moment, we need to see with new eyes.

As you look around, observe nature as if you were seeing it for the first time. Imagine yourself to be a careful and sensitive naturalist and feel a sense of awe at your discoveries, whether a thundering storm or a bug trundling across the floor. You may also explore the possibility of observing yourself and those around you with these same loving "new eyes" and perceive instances of newly discovered beauty everywhere.

Adopt the pace of nature, her secret is patience.

RALPH WALDO EMERSON

In this 21st century, patience is often not considered much of a virtue. We eat fast, sleep short, and commend ourselves for multi-tasking.

As an antidote to this frantic pace of modern life, we can practice adopting nature's pace by slowing down, for just a minute or half a minute at a time.

While eating, observe one slow mouthful, taking 10 or 20 seconds from the instant of the sandwich or food-laden fork rising to the mouth, to the swallowing of the well-chewed food.

While walking from place to place, choose one short section of your journey—even just walking across a single room—and take two or three seconds for each step, noticing the lifting, moving, and placing of the foot. Doing this even a few times each day will relax you and deepen your mindfulness meditation practice, even if this is all you do. This is an especially valuable exercise to do when out in nature, and you may be surprised at what you will perceive when traveling for a moment, at nature's pace.

We must all obey the great law of change. It is the most powerful law of nature.

EDMUND BURKE

OBSERVING NATURE, WE CAN see change happening almost before our eyes, as buds blossom into flowers or summer leaves appear to turn autumnal overnight. At other times, the pace of change is imperceptible, as when the Grand Canyon was carved across millions of years. Understanding this law of nature invites us to recognize how change also permeates our own lives.

Pay attention to changes large and small, both in nature and in your own life. Becoming aware of impermanence as it inevitably comes with change, provides us with an opportunity to be mindful in choosing our responses to the ephemeral quality of life.

You can choose to rail against this law of nature and create suffering for yourself. Or you can choose to observe the process of change in the natural world and in yourself, simply noting what is happening with interest and not adding an overlay of emotion.

To such an extent does nature delight and abound in variety that among her trees there is not one plant to be found which is exactly like another; and not only among the plants, but among the boughs, the leaves and the fruits, you will not find one which is exactly similar to another.

LEONARDO DA VINCI

THIS QUOTE REMINDS US that nature appears to love—or at least on some level, value—individuality and difference. To be mindful in nature is to perceive abundance laid out before us, as we delight in an infinity of unique attributes.

Be aware of trees, plants, and flowers with an appreciative eye for their differences, from the obvious to the almost imperceptible. Similarly, be aware of appreciating your own unique individuality.

As with nature, each person is different. By recognizing, without judgment, the variety of nature, you can begin to learn to be more accepting of yourself and others. Should feelings of judgment arise, simply refocus your total attention onto any natural object, and that moment of judgment will pass.

Much of the time, our mental stream of self-talk involves either comparing ourselves to others, or to the impossibly high standards that our culture tells us we should hold ourselves to.

Listen to da Vinci and spend a moment, every day, appreciating your own unique individuality, blemishes, quirks, and all. Notice judging thoughts that may arise ("Yes, I'm unique, but I really need to lose weight...") and gently let them go.

When the bird and the book disagree, believe the bird.

JOHN JAMES AUDUBON

MUCH OF THE TIME, our mental process involves placing more attention on what we are thinking *about* what we perceive, than on the *perception itself*.

When we see an object, whether a tree or a bird, or a slug, instead of simply observing the object, we engage in self-talk about it. Perhaps we label it. "That's a pine." Perhaps we judge it. "Ohh, a Red-headed Woodpecker, how beautiful." "A slug. Disgusting. Glad I didn't step on it."

When observing natural phenomena, try—at least some of the time—to simply see the colors of the flower, the sound of the waterfall, the feeling of wet leaves under bare feet. Apply that same keen observation to your mind and body. Study yourself and your reactions as though you were a rare and beautiful creature in the forest, observed by a careful and sensitive naturalist.

Love has no season.
It comes in the night of winter,
in the midday summer sun.
It has no reason to be born.
But I have never known it to be wasted.
Seasons change… And so, love's form.

FRIEDA FELDMAN

CHANGE IS A CONSTANT, like it or not. From the cells that are constantly being born and dying within our bodies, to the natural flow of seasons—change occurs in each moment. Some shifts are visible to us. Others are not. Whether the aging of our bodies or the emergence of new technologies in this increasingly complex world, whether we are happy or unhappy, eager or fearful, there's no way to put change on hold.

Nature, with its inexorable power and grace, offers a respite from tumultuous times in our lives, in the world. Here's an instant intervention you can use, if you are feeling overwhelmed.

Simply go outside and breathe. Eyes open or closed, breathe fully and slowly. Fill the lungs from the bottom up as the belly expands, then release as the belly contracts. As you feel the sensation of air entering and leaving your body, relax and enjoy the breath, clearing the mind of thoughts. Let the simplicity of nature bring clarity and depth to this moment.

As you do this for three minutes, a sense of spaciousness begins to flow with the breath, and with this spaciousness comes a choice. You can choose to bring this sense of serenity with you as you step back to the complexities of the moment. You can recognize that each moment is an opportunity to be mindfully present, whether outdoors or in.

This poem offers a reminder that, similar to nature, *love*—with its strength and joy—is also part of the changing world and is *everywhere*, if we are open to it.

A Final Note

We hope that the quotes, ideas, and suggestions in this book will help you to explore the remarkable opportunities for expanded awareness and personal growth available through mindfulness in nature.

As you practice opening your mind, your heart, and your spirit to the simplicity and immediacy of both mindfulness and nature, you'll find that you begin to carry within yourself a sense of spaciousness and centeredness. Know that each time you are *truly present* in the moment appreciating the natural world, you deepen and strengthen the mental pathways that connect you to this sense of well-being. Know that each time you *recall* how it feels to be present in this way, you're doing the same. Every time you do this, it becomes easier to do—more natural, as it were—as mindfulness in nature becomes "second nature" to you!

May your life be enriched by mindfulness in nature, bringing you moments of joy and memories to savor. May you also feel uplifted as you experience new ways of being present—one moment at a time.

About the Authors

❦

Dr. **Nina Smiley's** efforts to share mindfulness with *real* people in *real* lives when they *really* need it began when she co-authored *The Three Minute Meditator* with her beloved twin brother, David Harp, which was originally based on his master's thesis. First published in 1989, this informative and accessible book is now in its 5th edition and has been translated into 7 languages.

After earning her doctoral degree in psychology at Princeton University, Nina taught at the University of Maryland and worked for the American Psychological Association before her path led to Mohonk Mountain House in New Paltz, NY (www.mohonk.com), a unique Victorian castle resort founded in 1869, where she is now Director of Mindfulness Programming.

Nina's work in mindfulness has been seen in *O, the Oprah Magazine, Shape, Real Simple, Marie Claire,* and *The New York Times.* Nina leads programs and teaches private classes on mindfulness, wellness, and forest bathing. She delights in sharing simple and effective mindfulness meditation techniques that can be used *anytime* and *anywhere*, one moment at a time.

David Harp's work as a cognitive scientist involves studying the way in which the brain obtains and processes information, then uses that information to produce our words, our actions, and our emotions.

The author of more than two dozen books, including *Mindfulness To Go: How to Meditate While You're On the Move!* and *Neural Path Therapy: How to Change Your Brain's Response to Anger, Fear, Pain, and Desire*, a corporate speaker, and a professional musician, David travels the United States and the world helping organizations work more co-operatively, more creatively, and with less stress. But David never just lectures his audiences on the mysteries of the human brain; he also happens to be America's best-known and *fastest* harmonica teacher, with more than a million students to his credit, and the holder of the undisputed World's Record for Most-People-Taught-to-Play-Harmonica-at-One-Time (2,569)!

Thus David *combines* his two favorite mental disciplines—harmonica and cognitive psychology—into entertaining, interactive, and highly effective workshops for organizations ranging from Ben & Jerry's Ice Cream to Kraft Foods, from the Red Cross to Blue Cross, and for statewide corporate wellness events across the United

States. His work has been featured on television and radio programs including Good Morning America and National Public Radio and can be seen at www.thethreeminutemeditator.com

Both David and Nina delight in being outdoors. They have found, along with many others, comfort and support for living in an increasingly complex world from the profound simplicity of being mindful in nature.